Prepare
- To Be -
Hired

MARIOS ZENONOS

Contents

Preface: My Story

What makes you who you are? What situations and events in your life have shaped you? So much of our life experience impacts on our successes and our belief to achieve.

During my career, I have helped thousands of people on their journey to success and this guide condenses all of the experience and advice I have gained from over a decade working as a Talent Acquisition Head/Specialist. What drives me is a desire to educate, empower and elevate others, so they can achieve their career goals.

This stems from my experiences as a child. My school days were arduous to say the least. My teachers had little faith or belief in my capacity to be successful. How did I know this? It was the way in which they spoke to me, the feedback they gave my parents, and the way I was removed from my class to work in the special needs unit. The reasons for removing me from class were never explained to me and this only compounded the thoughts that I already felt about myself – "You are stupid. You are not good enough".

It was only later, aged 14, that I was privately assessed and diagnosed with dyslexia. It was discovered that I had the reading and writing age of an eight-year-old. It all made sense. I hated reading in front of the class, often walking out if my teacher asked me to. I failed most spelling tests and my handwriting was abysmal.

My parents could see that my school was continuing to fail me. Apart from being given an extra 15 minutes during my exams, very little support was offered, and it had a detrimental impact on my self-esteem. With regular calls home about my behaviour and lack of motivation in lessons, my parents decided to pay for me to attend a private tutor.

This is how I came to know Joyce, an 80-year-old retired teacher whose glare could send shivers down your spine. This frail-looking but fierce and determined lady kicked me into shape and showed me for the first time that I could be successful. She never allowed me to use my dyslexia as an excuse to fail or not do my best. She demanded excellence in every subject, at every moment, in every lesson - and God help me if I went to her sessions without doing my homework! I owe a lot of my success to Joyce; a woman who never gave up on me and who championed me until the end. As Joyce would say, "A grafter always wins, Marios" and she taught me that success comes to those who are prepared to put in the work.

My first job was as a recruitment associate; a sales job that meant I would be talking on the phone for 70% of the time. My dyslexia was still there, as was the shame. I saw my dyslexia as a hindrance and feared that if I was honest about it, employers would not give me opportunities and offer me work. I would arrive in the office an hour before opening time and leave two hours after closing just so I could go through all of my written correspondence and emails to check that my spelling was correct before sending.

I no longer carry that shame and have come to understand myself and my qualities better. I have overcome my internal battles through sheer graft and determination to make the most of the opportunities I have been given. My success at work and my expertise in my field has been recognised by some of the largest companies in recruitment and has enabled me to develop a fulfilling career helping others achieve their goals and ambitions. I hope with this guide, I can help you achieve yours too.

Introduction

I have been a Talent Acquisition Head/Specialist for over 10 years, interviewing thousands of applicants across a vast number of sectors including, finance, technology, and media. Throughout my career, I have provided interview preparation advice and support to people with various levels of skills and experience - from university graduates to chief executive officers.

In this guide I have encapsulated all my knowledge, experience, and advice for successful interviewing. The decision to purchase this guide is not enough to make you an interview master. It is the practiced determination of the preparation tasks and tips set out along the way which will help you to achieve your goals. We will cover the full interviewing process including interview preparation, confidence building, dealing with nerves and the benefits of psychometric analysis (personality measurements).

Some people live in the state of mind that others create for them through their perceptions. How you see yourself, and how others see you can be very different. While you read this guide, I would ask you to question yourself: Are you being the person you want to be, or the person you think others want you to be? Are you being your true self? Be in no doubt, professional panels can sniff out inauthenticity like dogs can sniff out bones.

Your CV has got you through the door. From this point onwards, your ability to convey and present your experience in a collaborative, professional and organised manner will lead you to the next step in your career. You may say, "But I am great at my job, why would they not hire me?". This precise thinking is just one of the barriers that prevent us from getting the jobs we want. Generally, as humans we lack the ability to link our lived experiences to the needs of the employer. This guide will show you how to convey your unique collection of experiences and qualities in an interview situation to land the job you desire and deserve.

Preparation is everything

In Daniel Kahneman's best-selling book '*Thinking, Fast and Slow*'[1], he talks about the two modes of thinking.

- System 1: Fast, instinctive and emotional.
- System 2: Slow, deliberative and logical.

We can use his theory to better prepare for our interviews and here is how:

Our minds are constantly calculating the world around us. To do this, the brain tries placing our habits and behaviours into a state of autopilot or 'System 1' (an unconscious, effortless and automatic way of operating). Every day I wake up, brush my teeth and have a coffee. This process is not something I think about, it is simply something that I do.

Our brains are lazy. It is easier to continue with the habits and behaviours currently available to us in 'System 1', whereas creative thinking is uncomfortable and requires the use of 'System 2' (a conscious, calculating and slower way of operating).

When you attend an interview unprepared, it requires a lot of 'System 2' thinking. During this process, your muscles tense up, your heart rate becomes elevated, your blood pressure

---

[1] Daniel Kahneman, '*Thinking, Fast and Slow*', (Penguin, 2012)

rises, and your pupils dilate. When you have fully prepared for the interview, your answers almost become automatic as the information has now become a part of your 'System 1' or automatic thinking.

Progressive Action learning

This book requires action. It is simple; read the content and complete the tasks. This book does not try to reinvent the wheel; instead, it uses problem-solving methods to identify areas for improvement and embeds verified interview techniques to help the reader reach their career goals.

My strong advice would be to spend the time required to complete the tasks outlined in this guide; to revisit them regularly and, where necessary, make additions based on new experiences. Take your time to re-read and run the tasks repeatedly until your understanding has moved to knowledge and embedded firmly in your 'System 1' thinking. Use and implement the teachings in this book to prepare for all future interviews. Run interview simulations, identify your needs, and focus on the chapters that will bring you the most value.

Chapter 1: What Interviewers Look For

If you find yourself wondering, "Why is this recruitment process so complicated?", consider this: it takes a significant investment of time and money to hire, train and integrate someone new into a business. Even the most experienced and skilled candidates will require a bedding in period to establish relationships with key colleagues/stakeholders, fully understand the details of the role and familiarise themselves with cultural nuances of the organisation they are joining.

A typical recruitment process could breakdown as follows:
- Advertising cost – this could be placing the role on a variety of websites, hiring a recruitment agency to identify suitable candidates, or utilising search engine marketing (SEM)/social media posts.
- Four hours of searching and shortlisting potential candidates by an internal recruiter.
- Two hours of initial 'stage one' phone calls to shortlisted candidates.
- One hour reviewing of all CV's shortlisted by the line manager.
- Four hours of 'stage two' interviewing by both the manager and the recruiter
- Two hours of 'stage three' interviewing by both a senior manager and manager
- Two hours to complete the job offer and on-boarding.
- Equipment cost
- HR time/cost
- Salary, NI, holidays, pension cost etc.

Since the repercussions of a bad hire are detrimental to any business, many companies will employ a robust application and interviewing process. This may take the form of a group interview where multiple candidates are invited to see how candidates approach tasks and interact with other people. Other recruitment process may involve multiple rounds of interviews or require the candidate to complete an exercise or make a presentation.

It is always worth keeping in mind that, no matter the format, the interviewer/s will consider their options based on four key factors:

1. Is the candidate qualified for the job?
2. Will this candidate fit within the company/team and the organisations' culture/ethos?
3. How prepared was this candidate throughout the interview process?
4. Is this person enthusiastic about this job and working for our company?

There are certain scenarios that can change which of these factors are more important than others. For example, in professions that require a particularly select set of skills, being able to demonstrate a high level of competency will be crucial in determining whether your candidacy is successful or not. One thing is certain, however; all four factors are being considered by the interviewer from the very beginning.

Take this example:

Candidate A is 80% qualified for the role and has made a good impression in previous contexts. However, Candidate A has shown some resistance and reluctance to learning from teammates in the group tasks and their enthusiasm is not noticed throughout the day.

Candidate B is 58% qualified for the role but has consistently shown enthusiasm and a keen interest throughout the interview process. Candidate B's commitment to their own development and learning is evident. They are enthusiastic about meeting the team and wish to learn from the people around them.

An experienced manager would weigh up their options based on the following: Candidate A would be very good at completing tasks quickly with little supervision but is not a team player and this could cause unrest and discord within the team/with other colleagues. Candidate B, on the other hand, would require more supervision for the first six months of employment but has demonstrated a willingness to work on self-improvement and has a personality and enthusiasm which colleagues will find uplifting. Candidate B will work hard and, with the right guidance, will work smarter. In other words, Candidate A presents a quick-fix solution while Candidate B is an investment.

You might think that knowledge and experience would give Candidate A the edge over Candidate B in our example but attitude can account for 30% of the decision process. In interview scoring systems used by some HR professionals, candidates are typically marked against each question with a score of 1-5 in both knowledge and attitude. Using such a method in this example, Candidate A is an 80% fit for the role while Candidate B has a combined score of 98%. Skills can be learned; attitudes are a mind-set. Make sure you are presenting the correct attitude to your prospective employers.

With all of this in mind, make sure you have researched the role and the company thoroughly ahead of your interview. You should visit their website, review their corporate literature to find out what services/products they offer and what the company's values are. Being able to reference a recent piece of corporate news or activity during your interview demonstrates an interest and enthusiasm in the business that goes beyond merely reading the job specification.

Bear in mind also that interviews are a two-way process. While the employer will be seeing if you would be the best fit or candidate for the job, you will be doing the same and asking yourself, "Can I see myself working here? Is this the job I really want?".

Time to prepare:
Ensure you have as much information on the recruitment process as possible prior to interview:

- Do you know what format the interview will take? (E.g. is it a group interview with other candidates, a panel interview or one-to-one?)
- Will there be multiple stages? If so, how many?
- Have you been told who you will be meeting?
- Will you be required to complete any tasks either on the day or in advance as part of the interview process?
- Will there be any psychometric testing?

If you do not know the answer to any of the above questions, you must ask the organiser before the interview so that you can prepare yourself accordingly.

Chapter 2: The Value of Self-Assessment

Any successful interview is going to require you to sell yourself. While it is obviously important to convey your professional/academic achievements, experience and enthusiasm for the role on offer, it's just as important to present your personal qualities, attributes and attitude.

Consider the following questions:
- How do you want to be perceived?
- How do you perceive yourself?
- How do others perceive you?

Speak to people you know and ask them the following questions:
- What would you say are my personal qualities, skills, or attributes?
- What characteristics of mine do you find unique or intriguing?
- What would you say are my areas for development?

Ensure you ask a variety of people you have previously worked with and/or currently work with and ask for their honest feedback. One idea could be to create an anonymous form. This way you can be certain that the feedback you receive will be more likely to be honest. Be prepared; sometimes the responses may feel like criticisms but what you do with the feedback can and will open your mind to new personal development needs which can only help you better prepare for success.

Psychometric Profiling
Psychometric analysis is a tool used by many companies to identify the key strengths and development areas of their staff and prospective candidates. Usually, it is conducted via a Personal Profile Analysis (PPA) to access an individual's

inner workplace behavioural style, motivations, fears, drives and coping mechanisms. Its use has grown in popularity in recent years with over 75% of the UK's Top 100 companies and HR recruitment specialists employing some form of psychometric testing.[2]

Self-understanding is crucial to self-growth. It is only when we allow ourselves the time to truly reflect on who we are, what makes us tick, and look deeper into our own personality traits that we are able to begin a journey into developing our standard way of operating. I have personally and professionally found psychometric analysis is an especially useful tool for understanding self-behaviour.

I was first psychometrically analysed when I was a team member and found the results both staggering and enlightening. My report explained how I cared too much about what others thought about me and this behaviour had prevented me from working within upper management. It was due to this insight that I actively changed my behaviour to align with my goals.

I use the Thomas International DISC assessment which looks at four contributing factors of an individual's personality and behavioural patterns: Dominance, Influence, Steadiness and Compliance. An individual's personality is comprised of all four of DISC factors. The most prominent factor indicates the way a person is most likely to act.

---

[2] Guy Thornton, 'Is there a proven scientific link between psychometric testing and hiring the best people?', Test Candidates.com, 1 November 2020, https://www.testcandidates.com/magazine/is-there-a-proven-scientific-link-between-psychometric-testing-and-hiring-the-best-people/

Figure 1: DISC Profile Understanding *(Source: Thomas International)*

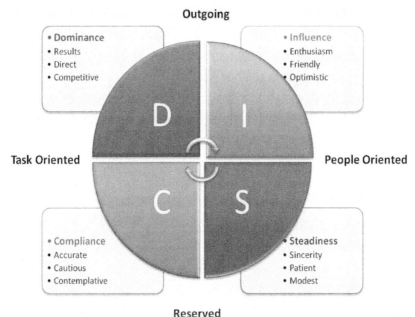

Outgoing

- Dominance
- Results
- Direct
- Competitive

- Influence
- Enthusiasm
- Friendly
- Optimistic

Task Oriented

People Oriented

- Compliance
- Accurate
- Cautious
- Contemplative

- Steadiness
- Sincerity
- Patient
- Modest

Reserved

High Dominance Personality

This highly resourceful, determined style of personality responds best to high-pressure environments and challenging circumstances. Everything becomes a competition. When there is little to no challenge, High Dominance Personalities quickly lose interest. Being goal and result oriented makes a High D personality to be less considerate of people's feeling. This makes their interactions with others very direct and can be perceived as blunt or rude. However, they have a deep respect for authority.

Basic fears: Failure

Company Value: Results Oriented

Motivated by: Power

Management style: Direct

Communication style: Delegating

High Influence Personality

Highly emotionally intelligent personalities. They feel relationships are more important than results. Fantastic listeners and social butterflies who are able to effortlessly engage with someone new and quickly build a strong bond. Such people are known for acting on impulse and make decisions based on gut feeling rather than the facts. These highly persuasive personalities yearn for everyone to like them and may struggle when applying discipline.

Basic fears: Rejection
Company Value: Building relationships
Motivated by: Recognition
Management style: Motivating
Communication style: Conversational

High Steadiness Personality

This very conservative personality is highly professional in the workplace. A controlled human that sees the value in listening before speaking. They build deep, meaningful relationships with a handful of people and are willing to drop everything when those relationships are in need. Stability and job/life security is a large driving force and therefore they do not trust easily. High steadiness personalities feel uncomfortable with change, particularly when the change is abrupt or unexpected.

Basic fears: Insecurity
Company Value: Support
Motivated by: Security
Management style: Organisational
Communication style: Listening

High Compliance Personality

These peaceful shape-shifters can adapt themselves to any situation apart from one: conflict. Being non-aggressive, they are eager and able to follow direction, making this cautious individual a shrewd rule enforcer. Uncomfortable when making decisions, high compliance personalities take their time and ensure all due diligences and information is received before committing one decision. As soon as conflict arises, high compliance moves to avoid the situation. They experience great fear to be in the firing line of a workplace conflict.

Basic fears: Conflict
Company Value: Technical/quality/standards
Motivated by: Standard operating procedures
Management style: By the book / rule enforcement
Communication style: Writing

Time to prepare:

After reading all four of the personalities, consider which one most closely resembles you. Combine this information with the feedback you have received from others to identify your main personality traits and, if necessary, try to actively alter your behaviour to align with your goals and ambitions.

Chapter 3: Building Confidence

"Self-confidence is the first requisite to great undertakings."

- Samuel Johnson

As an interview and life coach, I estimate around 90% of the people I have worked with suffer from a lack of confidence or low self-esteem and can find it difficult to overcome, especially when preparing for an interview scenario. You may feel this applies to you too so I have included in this chapter methods for building confidence and counteracting the negative thoughts that can be a barrier to success at interview.

According to the psychologist Barbara Markway, "Studies have shown that our genetic makeup affects the amount of certain confidence-boosting chemicals our brain can access. Serotonin, a neurotransmitter associated with happiness, and oxytocin, the 'cuddle hormone', can both be inhibited by certain genetic variations. Somewhere between 25 to 50 percent of the personality traits linked to confidence may be inherited."[3]

Although there is evidence to suggest there is a link between genetic makeup and a lack of confidence, do not use this reason to say, "Hey, that must be me, and there is nothing I can do about it" - because there is!

When lacking confidence, we may search for a boost. This could come in the form of watching a motivational video,

---

[3] Barbara Markway, '5 Reasons People Have Low Self-Confidence', Psychology Today, 7 December 2018, https://www.psychologytoday.com/gb/blog/shyness-is-nice/201812/5-reasons-people-have-low-self-confidence

posting a picture on social media to gain likes, or speaking to a trusted friend. All these are used to temporarily stimulate chemicals in your brain associated with happiness. This quick fix is great but short-lived as the root cause has yet to be identified or acted upon. Soon your brain will return to normal, and you will go back to feeling the same as you did before.

Low self-confidence is difficult to overcome but it helps to start at the source. This may be related to bad experiences in your past, a difficult upbringing or circumstances which have left you feeling out of control/deflated.

The key to self-confidence is knowing and understanding yourself and *who you are*. Often a lack of confidence stems from a fear of something. One method to identify the source of your low self-confidence is to approach it as an organisation would a manufacturing problem: by using root cause analysis.

The Five Whys

The "five whys" is a problem-solving methodology originally founded in the 1930s by Japanese industrialist Sakichi Toyoda.

The building blocks of this methodology is to ask yourself "why" five times until the root of the problem reveals itself. Once you have made yourself aware of the root cause, usually the solution becomes clear and then you may act accordingly. You can approach almost any problem with this method and find by interrogating it, the solution can reveal itself as a matter of process.

Example:
Problem – I lack confidence for my interview next week.
Why?

"Because I get nervous."

Why?

"Because I don't feel prepared."

Why?

"Because I don't feel I have all of the information."

Why?

"The recruiter has not sent me enough details."

Why?

"Because I have not asked."

Counter measures: Ask the recruiter for more information. Then detail an action plan for the coming days to familiarise yourself with all aspects of the job specification, company, and interviewers.

All problems have a root cause and while not all problems will have a firm and fixed solution, by practicing the "five whys" we can begin to manage the issues around it.

Word replacement

In Allen Carr's *'Easy Way to Stop Smoking'*[4], he outlines a method to alter the negative association with "giving up" smoking by using a simple yet powerful brain training technique. In the days you stop smoking, someone will offer you a cigarette. Replace the words "no thanks, I quit", with, "no thanks, I don't need it anymore". The words "I quit", suggest to the brain that you have 'tapped out' or 'failed'. By using word replacement, you can alter your brains understanding for the lack of nicotine from a negative to a positive connotation.

When I first wanted to lose weight, I went to the gym every day. When I got home, I would indulge in a heavy dinner, three

---

[4] Allen Carr, *'Easy Way to Stop Smoking'* (Penguin, 2015)

chocolates and a packet of crisps. I was not losing weight.

I decided it was time to try a diet. I managed to cut down on the heavy dinner, and the crisps were easy to give up. However, anything associated with chocolate was my kryptonite. I would squirm every time someone would offer me these delicious treats and find myself caving into temptation.

I then discovered I could apply Carr's technique through linguistics and word replacement. Every time someone would offer me chocolates or cakes, I would put my hand up with my palm facing the temptation and say, "No thanks, I don't like chocolates". Eventually after repeating this at every turn, I found that my addiction to chocolate and all things sweet, subsided. I was now in control of my addiction.

Use this word association technique to encourage your brain to have more confidence. We all know the feeling when our confidence begins to slip; that gut-wrenching heaviness in the pit of our stomach, the quivers in our voice, the adrenaline being pumped around our body. It is time to tame the beast and change the language we use about ourselves.

Impostor syndrome
This is a psychological pattern in which an individual doubts their skills, talents or accomplishments and has an internalised fear of being exposed as a 'fraud'. The term 'imposter syndrome' was first used by psychologist Suzanna Imes and Pauline Rose Clance in the 1970s paper *'Psychotherapy: Theory, Research & Practice'*.

Impostor syndrome is most common in people who are interviewing for a job that will move their status from team member to team manager, or student to worker. Nonetheless, impostor syndrome has affected many people in their daily work lives and can negatively impact your career prospects if you do not acknowledge it and deal with it early on.

A survey by Roar Training revealed 96% of respondents said they had imposter syndrome and over half (53%) said they had turned down work opportunities due to a lack of confidence[5]. So, if you feel this may apply to you, take comfort in knowing you are not alone and that there are steps you can take to reduce these feelings of inferiority.

Ditch the 'Perfectionist Misconception'

Being wrong about a situation or issue is OK. Do not operate under misguided conceptions like "I should know all the answers" or "if I ask for help, they will know I don't know what I am doing". You have a right to be wrong and it is ok to ask for assistance.

Think Positive

Think positive and visualise your success. You may find yourself thinking "I'm not worthy" and yet you are here because someone saw something in you that you cannot see yet. When that wave of uncertainty hits, affirm your right to be there, tell yourself "I deserve to be here; I can do this; I trust the process of progression".

---

[5] Beau Jackson, *'Imposter syndrome pervades the workplace'*, HR Magazine.co.uk, 24 May 2021, https://www.hrmagazine.co.uk/content/news/imposter-syndrome-pervades-the-workplace

Time to prepare:
Describe yourself in the best way possible. Create a sentence that you will memorise forever. This mantra will act as your own personal fear-neutralising agent. When fear strikes, repeat the sentence. Eventually your brain will learn that when you say your power sentence there is nothing to fear, and you have this under control.
For example, mine is: "I am a powerful & courageous. I do not feel fear in taking control of my life. Fear does not stop me from achieving my goals."

Chapter 4: Dealing With Nerves

"Nothing diminishes anxiety faster than action."
-   Walter Anderson

It is perfectly natural to feel anxious or nervous before an interview. A study carried out in 2019 stated that 73% of people felt more nervous at interview than at the doctors or dentist! Feeling nervous is a natural, human response to a situation that can feel threatening.

The emotional part of our brains controls the 'Fight, Flight or Freeze' response system. This is a reflex embedded in the brain from the days of the cave man to protect us from danger. Unfortunately, this response system cannot tell the difference between an interview situation and a sabre-toothed tiger sprinting towards us.

Before interview, some of us go through an array of emotions. These emotions all sit within the three stages of anxiety.
- Stage 1: Calming stage. Here is where we want to be.
- Stage 2: The blurry stage. Here, mind blanks occur, the "ums" and "ers" increase and it becomes difficult to listen to questions and respond accurately.
- Stage 3: The panic stage. All systems, red alert! Activate 'fight/flight/freeze' mode!

Anxiety tends to rise the closer you come to the time for interview. You may find, however, that once the interview starts, your anxiety levels begin to drop. If we walk into an interview at the peak of stage two, it will take time before calming down and comfortably responding within the stage one parameter. By the time the stage two anxiety has subsided, it may be too late; you have already given your first impression and answered two interview questions.

The most efficient way to counteract these emotions is to incorporate coping mechanisms before the anxiety rises to stage two.

Figure 2: The Three Stages of Interview Anxiety *(source: www.EnterView.co.uk)*

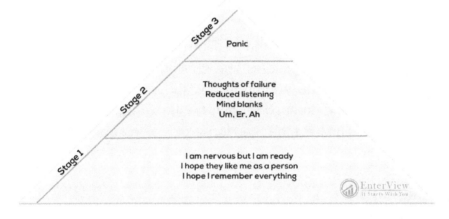

Why do we get nervous?

According to the *'The Chimp Paradox'*, a mind management model created by Professor Steve Peters[6], our human brains are metaphorically in battle with our "inner chimp" which lives in our limbic system (the emotional side of the brain) that thinks and acts without our permission. The chimp is driven by primal needs and fears which can overwhelm us if we allow it. We are unable to "wrestle the chimp" as it is five times stronger than a human, but we can distract and/or manage the chimp into submission.

---

[6] Professor Steve Peters, *Chimp Paradox* (Vermilion, 2012)

So, how do we do this?

Preparedness
By far the most powerful anti-anxiety medication is your preparedness. Being ready for the situation gives you a sense of control. Being prepared means you have a plan for all contingencies. Nothing beats knowing everything about the interviewer, company and possible questions that will be asked at interview.

Tongue twisters
You may be familiar with the "red lorry, yellow lorry" or "unique New York" tongue twisters. The challenge is to see whether you can repeat the sentence quickly without slurring your words. Focusing on such tongue twisters before an interview is one way to distract the emotional side of the brain and calm the nerves.

Chewing gum
Try chewing gum before an interview to calm your nerves. Chewing gum suppresses your fight/ flight/freeze response system, deceiving the brain into believing you are eating and therefore safe. Just remember to throw it in the bin before the interview starts!

Lightly biting your tongue
Dry mouth is a real problem when presenting in front on an interview panel. There are several ways to overcome this. Having a glass of water helps although this does not activate your salivary glands meaning you will likely need a jug of water (and drinking that much water has its own consequences). Try lightly biting the middle of your tongue or cheek, this will active your salivary glands and sort out your dry mouth.

Breathe deep and visualise the 'win'

Short breaths are a fast route to stage three in the anxiety model ('Panic'). Close your eyes, take 3–6 deep long breaths and visualise your interview being a success.

According to Dr Martin Pauls, a professor of psychiatry at the University of California, "taking deep slow breaths convinces our minds that we are already in a state of relaxation"[7].

Hold a power item. A power item can be any small item that you can metaphorically pour your nervousness. The idea behind the power item is that it acts as a sort of "comfort blanket" which helps anchor you in the moment while you are presenting, enabling you to focus your mind and relax into the flow of your words. Just ensure that it is something unobtrusive (e.g. a pen or pencil) or small enough to be concealed (e.g. a pebble or coin).

Power poses

In a 2012 TED Talk by Kate Torgovnick May, she discusses nonverbal expressions of power and dominance. She explains, "When we are feeling confident and powerful, we position our bodies in an open stance, whereas, when we are feeling powerless, we tend to close up, hunch down and make ourselves small".

There is evidence to suggest our nonverbal expressions not only influence how other people see us, but they can affect how we think and feel about ourselves too; by simply changing the way we stand can have a positive physiological as well as

---

[7] Erin Brodwin, *'The Way You Breathe Could Be Affecting Your Emotions',* Science Alert.com, 27 July 2016, https://www.sciencealert.com/the-way-you-breath-could-change-your-emotions

psychological impact.

According to Torgovnick May, people who stood in a 'hero pose' (hands on hips, chest and head facing up) for two minutes experienced significant physiological changes to the body and mind. The results of the experiment showed a 20% increase in testosterone levels (the hormone linked to the feeling of power) and a 25% decrease in cortisol levels (a hormone linked to stress). When people were forced to use closed postures (i.e. arms crossed), the effects were reversed. Try using the hero pose before the interview for a boost in confidence.

Time to prepare:
Test all six confidence boosters to see which works for you. Be sure to use and implement the coping mechanisms when you begin to feel nervous and eventually your body will become accustom to being more confident in future.

Chapter 5: First Impressions and Behaviours

"We have two seconds to make a good impression and, in that time, people will judge our level of success, our trustworthiness, our friendliness and our social status."
- MIT Study by the Harvard School of Health Sciences[8]

First impressions count. Do not be fooled into thinking otherwise. From the first interaction you have, whether by email, phone/video call or face-to-face, first impressions often determine whether someone is willing to spend more time learning about you or not.

According to the economist John Kenneth Galbraith, "When faced with the choice between changing one's mind and proving there is no need to do so, almost everyone gets busy on the proof."[9] Recovering from a bad impression is a Herculean task. Suffice to say, it is more productive to work on our first impressions than try to prove ourselves later down the line.

To give yourself the best chance of making a good first impression, it is important for you to know and understand how you present the qualities you have to others, and shrewdly identify any areas for improvement *(see chapter 2)*.

Top Tips:

1. Be punctual
I would always advise that you turn up early to an interview.

---

[8] P. Borkenau, S. Brecke, C. Mottig, and M. Paelecke, *'Extraversion Is Accurately Perceived After a 50-Ms Exposure to a Face'*, Journal of Research in Personality, August 2009.
[9] Olivia Fox Cabane, *The Charisma Myth: How to Engage, Influence and Motivate People* (Penguin Books Ltd, 2013) p102

This shows good manners and organisation. Being late or "just in the nick of time" portrays you as someone who is disorganised, who will not meet deadlines or is an excuse maker. Not only does this have an impact on the first impression you create but also leaves you flustered before the interview. Equally you do not want to turn up *too* early - I would recommend no more than 15 minutes.

2. Be aware of the receptionist

Your interview starts from the moment you enter the building. Receptionists are powerful influencers. As front-line welcoming staff, receptionists are great at building relationships and reading body language. If the recruiting manager has a good relationship with the receptionist, they will listen to their first impressions of you and ask for their opinion. In the past, when receptionists would call me to meet a candidates for interview, they would immediately give me their first impression feedback, whispering "I like this one" or "this one is a bit weird" or "John is here to see you, 'he thinks'...He is uncertain of who he is meeting". Your first impressions start at the door, so be aware and be on your game from the moment you enter the building.

3. Do not offend the senses

Be careful not to overwhelm a panel's sense of smell. It is often tempting to use your favourite perfume, aftershave, or sprays. Overdoing it will flood the senses of the interviewers, making it difficult for them to focus on the marvel that is you!

The opposite of overloading with fragrance, will of course be smelling of bad odours. Needless to say, no one wants to work with someone who smells bad.

Finally, if you are a smoker, do not smoke before you go into an interview. The smell of stale cigarettes is intolerable to non-smokers. You may think the interviewer cannot smell it, but believe you me, they can, and this may put an employer off.

Maintaining good hygiene shows you care about yourself and

the people around you. Be sure to visit the bathroom when you arrive to ensure you look just as sharp as you did when you left your home.

4. Be enthusiastic

Show an interest in the person you meet but do not get too personal. Do not be afraid to show that you are excited to learn more about them and the prospect of working within their organisation. In my experience, 90% of recruiters perceive enthusiasm and passion as a charming sign of strength and will often shortlist a candidate as a result.

5. Non-Verbal Communication

A good handshake, a warm smile, eye contact and body language are simple things that combine to make up good non-verbal first impressions. Good eye contact shows you are trustworthy, attentive and a good listener. Good posture shows you are confident, enthusiastic and have a thirst for the job. Wearing the appropriate attire shows respect for the company and the people you are meeting.

During an interview you must be mindful of your body language. There are certain actions and postures which can create a negative impression. For example, face touching may be associated with dishonesty, crossed limbs can suggest a defensive and/or an unapproachable demeanour, and fidgeting creates the impression of boredom.

Mirroring the interviewer's body language subconsciously indicates that you are on the same page. Also, using hand gestures to express your point of view demonstrates a level of passion.

6. Opening questions

When you first meet the interviewer, they are likely to ask you several opening questions to break the ice. The first three sentences can determine the overall interview mood. Avoid one-word answers, be polite and show an interest. Your responses will show them a lot about you your personality and attributes. Remember to think about how you would like to be perceived.

You may be asked if you found the building ok and a good response would be, "I arrived with time to spare. I only live X minutes away / miles away. Do you live far from here?". Showing an interest in the person interviewing you is key. You could tell them how impressed you have been with the interview process so far and perhaps ask how long they have worked there. Whatever happens, be authentic. Ask genuine questions and listen to the answers with the intent to understand more about who they are as a person and the organisation more broadly.

Time to prepare:
Practice professional verbal and non-verbal communication. There is a fine line between getting this right and getting this wrong. Learning to show your personable qualities through your actions without having to verbally explain them is the key to a successful first impression.

Take note of what has been covered so far and use it to plan the best possible first impression for your next interview. Look at the results of your anonymous feedback *(see chapter 2)* and use this to help you. You might find it useful to create a checklist and go through this as you travel to interview.

Chapter 6: Interview Preparation

"By failing to prepare, you are preparing to fail."
-    Benjamin Franklin

Preparation is key to the success of any interview. You must be prepared beyond doubt so that when you are presented with the opportunity to prove your worth to any company, you are able to fire off your answers with confidence and pride. There are no short routes to preparation; no 'cheat codes' or 'key to the safe'. If you are unwilling to put in the work at the beginning, you are less likely to reap the rewards at the end.

There are many types of interview styles, all of which are designed to test your ability to perform within a set job role. Ultimately, the employer is trying to gain a clear image of your career history, motivations, skills, and personal characteristics.

Let's break this down.

Always start with the job specification. It is there for a reason and therefore you should know and understand what this is prior to interview. To have reached the interview stage, you will, of course, have used this to form part of your application.

Prior to considering the types of questions you may be asked, take a deep dive into each criterion outlined in the job description.

The job specification outlines the needs of the employer. Whilst reading the job description, consider the following questions:

- What skills are required of me to be successful in each criteria listed?
- Have I done this part of the job before? What examples can I use?
- Do I have the required qualifications stated as essential?
- What desirable experience do I have?
- What is my USP (unique selling point)?

Print out a copy and highlight your strengths and areas of development using two different coloured highlighters, then number each section and write down what experience you have had - with examples - to show how you have met each criterion. Not everyone will meet all criteria, therefore knowing and understanding the areas you need to develop prior to interview and how you intend to meet these elements of the job specification is vital.

Preparing your achievement examples

Determining your career achievements can be difficult, especially when considering your own work life. Using the following questions to narrow down your achievements will help you to create your answers:

- What problem did you identify? How did you solve it?
- What processes did you implement to improve products/services/workflow efficiency?
- Have you saved time/money for the company? How? When?
- Did you receive special recognition? What did they say?
- Have you received any company awards?

Typical interview questions

A well-prepared interviewer will have a mixture of competency interview questions and classic interview questions based on the job specification and their requirements. You will need to do the same for your practice runs.

Competency interview questions

Competency interview questions are designed to extract real life examples from your working career. The employer wants you to demonstrate your work experience, skills, and behaviours from previous employments.

Examples:
"Name a time you have had to deal with a difficult customer? How did you deal with this situation and what was the outcome?"
"Name a time you have delivered exceptional customer service. What did you do and what was the outcome?"
"Tell me about a time you have had to correct your superior. What was the situation and how was it received?"

Classic interview questions

Classic interview questions are considered traditional and are believed to be less effective at obtaining the information required from a candidate. Classic interview questions are open and subjective and therefore focus on self-image as opposed to seeking to understand how a candidate may behave in various work situations. Nonetheless, these questions are still being used today and you will need to prepare accordingly.

Examples:
"What are your strengths and weakness/areas for development?"
"What do think you can bring to the role?"
"Tell me about yourself"

Competency Interview Questions

It would be a waste of your time to simply search 'competency interview questions' online. Although you may find thousands of possible examples, these may not be directly relevant to the job you are applying for.

The job specification contains all the clues you need to extract an accurate line of questioning that the interviewer may ask you. If you have received a short job specification, which makes it impossible to glean this information, consider calling the recruiter to ask for further details.

From the job specification, you will need to produce a list of up to 11 possible questions: two classic and nine competency questions. The job specification can be broken down into three candidate attribute categories:

- Personality and communication suitability
- Skills and role suitability
- Company and team culture suitability

To create accurate competency interview questions, you will need to properly extract them from both the candidate attributes categories and the job specification.

Each question will need to be laid out using the following format:

"Tell me about a time you have [faced a situation]; how did you deal with it and what was the result?"

Example:

Job role – Bank Manager

Duties involve:

Working alongside stakeholders and playing a key role in implementing a new customer service strategy.

1. Analysing current processes and finding new solutions.
2. Keeping in line with our company values – "Honesty, Service and Creativity"

Extracted competencies questions:

1. Tell me about a time you have dealt with a difficult stakeholder. What was the situation, how did you manage it and what was the outcome?
2. Tell me about a time you have analysed and improved a pre-existing process. What was the situation, how did you manage it and what was the outcome?
3. Tell me about a time you have delivered exceptional service. What was the situation, how did you manage it and what was the outcome?

How to answer competency interview questions

All competency-based questions can be answered using SAR: Situation, Action, and Result.

Figure 3: The SAR Framework (*source*:
www.EnterView.co.uk)

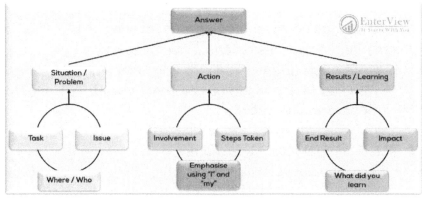

Using this framework, an example SAR answer could look like this:

Situation: While working at [Company X], a customer wanted to return an item that had broken within the first week of purchase. When I first answered the call, the customer was frustrated and angry. He immediately asked for my manager.

Action: I calmly explained that I could help much faster than putting him on hold to call over my manager. He agreed and proceeded to direct his complaint to me.

Result: After five minutes of listening to the customer, I refunded the item, apologised for the inconvenience, and sent him the item for free to make up for lost time. The customer was happy and rated my service 'five stars'.

Preparing your competency interview answers
To start your preparation, you will need to list your work history achievements and align them to each candidate attribute category: personality and communication, skill and role,

company and team culture. It helps to re-read your CV a few times before creating your achievements, just to jog your memory.

Creating an achievement-based answer is formulated using the three SAR components. Simply put, what did you do, how did you do it, and what were the quantifiable results?

Examples:

Personality and Communication
-   I was tasked with training all line managers on a new system which was being rolled out across the company. At the time most managers had been long-standing employees and were used to the old way of doing things. To ensure the successful roll-out, I identified the managers with influence and strategically approached them first. In doing so, I was able to gain their support, using their influence to roll out the new system more effectively. After a few meetings and strategic broadcast emails, all line managers were on board and eager to learn as the system proved to be more efficient and less time-consuming.

Skills and Role fit
-   When I first started at [Company X], there was no automatic candidate tracking system in place. In fact, [Company X] was still using emails to manage all their recruitment needs. I researched, implemented and rolled out a brand-new recruiting system that organised candidates into categories, making the search function more efficient. All the senior staff now had more control and an accurate understanding of their recruiting needs. Recruitment within this company is now cost and time efficient.

Cultural fit
-   Before answering this question, you must take into consideration the values of the company you are applying for. If the company values are "honesty, integrity and insight", try to create answers based around these factors.

Powerful words and phrases

Ensure you incorporate 'power words' into your competency answers as they will bring your answers to life and show your candidature in a positive and engaging light. For example:

Figure 4: Power words (*source*: www.EnterView.co.uk)

Authority	Excitement	Teamwork	Results Orientated
Absolute	Bold	Flexible	Deliverable
Comprehensive	Exciting	Reliable	Accountable
Guaranteed	Fascinating	Responsible	Solution
Ironclad	Intriguing	Collaborative	Proactive

Use positive, affirmative language when talking about yourself and your work. For example, say "I will do my best" and "I believe I can" instead of "I will try my best" and "I think I can". The difference may seem subtle but "I will try" and "I think" in this context suggests doubt, whereas "I will" and "I can" instils a sense of confidence and intention.

Time to prepare:
Competency questions
1. Using the questions you have extracted based on the job specification, put your answers together using the SAR methodology (Situation, Action, and Result) and employ the use of power words

2. Memorise your answers and go through these at every opportunity. Say them out loud and really focus on what you are saying and how you are saying it. If necessary, practice in front of friends and family. Memorising your answers gives you fluency at interview. You will be able to answer questions with ease, leaving the employer feeling confident and comfortable you are right for the job.

Classic Interview Questions

Here are the top three most common classic interview questions:

1. Tell me about yourself.
2. Why should we hire you?
3. What are your strengths and weaknesses/areas of development?

"Tell me about yourself"

The answer to this question requires practice, repetition, and memorising.

This question is the typical show starter of all interviews. Although this is an open-ended and broad question, it is a great opportunity to sell yourself as the right candidate for the job.

You want to keep this answer to a maximum of 60 seconds, whilst providing valuable information in a confident, effortless, and clear manner. The words should flow off the tongue. If you find yourself using "er", then you have not practised enough.

Figure 5: The 60 second Framework
(source:www.EnterView.co.uk)

As indicated in Figure 4, you can approach this answer in the following format:

"I am a *[job title]* with over *[years of experience]* working within *[type of companies (e.g. global, small, medium, in-house, agency) and/or sector (e.g. finance, technology, consultancy)]*. In my recent career history, I performed/achieved/specialise in *[job, achievement or purpose relevant to current interview]."*

You need to be clear about the impact you have had within an organisation.

Time to prepare

Set a 60 second timer and answer each question within the given time. This will give you the opportunity to practice an answer that is to the point and has the intended impact. You may need to try more than once but that's ok; it is about progression not perfection.

To be clear, the 60 second timer is only intended for practice purposes. You do not have to stick to 60 second during the interview. Take your time be aware of the speed and tone of your voice.

The "Curveball" Questions

To be fully prepared for an interview, we must take into consideration questions that we have not rehearsed for. After all, we are not fortune-tellers and despite your carefully prepared analysis, the job description may not fully outline every aspect of the role.

"Curveball" questions could be standard competency or classic interview questions asking about skills that were not outlined on the job specification. This category of interview questions will either be open and non-specific or hypothetical scenario-based:

Open and non-specific
- What gets you up in the morning?
- Would you rather be liked or feared?
- Where does your boss think you are right now?

Hypothetical
- If you were a clock, what time would you show and why?
- If you could choose any superpower, what would it be and why?
- If you could be any fictional character, who would you choose and why?

These questions are meant to provoke thought. They are designed to test the candidate's capacity to think on their feet and shed insight into their ethical merits and problem-solving skills.

Consider the question, "Where does your boss think you are right now?" The interviewer is looking for your ethical decision-making skills. If you answer, "on my lunch break", "on sick leave" or "on a client's site", they will see this as a negative reflection of your candour and naturally assume you would behave similarly at a new place of work.

Being authentic, ethical, and honest in your responses to questions is key. Avoid cheesy, off-the-cuff answers and be sure that you do not say anything that puts your integrity into question.

Pace and Tone
Take your time and embrace the pause
When you answer questions, TAKE YOUR TIME! Many people fall for the notion that answering questions immediately gives extra points. This is a misconception. Taking a short pause before answering shows the interviewer you have actively listened to the question and considered your reply. When the interviewer sees you are calm, collected, and reflective in your responses, they will associate this behaviour with the way in which you work.

Allowing a maximum of five seconds of silence prior to responding to questions allows you to gather your thoughts and prevents "ums" and "erms" from slipping into your answer. Time fillers such as "um, erm" are often used to allow your brain to find the right words or remember something you have temporarily forgotten. The frequency of these fillers usually increases when discussing matters you are unclear about. Rather than rush into a response, if you need time to consider your answer then be candid and say, "I'm just going think about this question before I respond". This shows that you are thoughtful and reflective.

Be sure not to overdo the silent pauses otherwise it becomes a little uncomfortable for the interviewer and you may begin panicking over the length of time that it has taken you to respond. If you need to buy yourself a bit more thinking time, repeat the question back to the interviewer before going into the details of your answer.

Often when people are nervous, the pace of their speech increases without them realising. Slowing down your words helps you to gather your thoughts, keeps the attention of your audience, builds curiosity, and gives the interviewer time to process the information you are presenting. However, if you overdo it, there is a danger your responses become monotone and boring.

Successful public speakers engage their audiences' attention by constantly altering their words per minute. They will speak "faster" when using words of passion or urgency and "slower" when using words of wisdom or innovation. They will also employ frequent use of short pauses to emphasise points and allow their audience a moment to soak up the information. Research suggests the average person pauses between 0.20 to 1.00 second per minute of speaking, whereas good public speakers will use up to 10 pauses lasting up to three seconds or more[10].

Once you have mastered this technique your communication will improve significantly and will help you when dealing with people in any situation. You will find that others will understand and consider your point of view more often and engage more with the ideas and concepts you put forward.

---

[10] Estelle Campione and Jean Veronis, 'A Large-Scale Multilingual Study of Silent Pause Duration', University of Provence, France, 2002, https://www.isca-speech.org/archive_open/sp2002/sp02_199.pdf

Figure 6: Pace and Tone (*source*: www.EnterView.co.uk)

	Speaking at a <u>fast</u> pace	Speaking at a <u>slow</u> pace
PROS	• Good for driving a point of urgency or call to action	• Builds suspense • Gives time for others to absorb and understand the information • Gives your mind time to form the next sentence, reducing 'Ums' and 'Ahs'
CONS	• Higher likelihood of misunderstanding or missing details • Higher likelihood of 'Ums' and 'Ahs'	• If kept up for prolonged periods of time the speaker may sound monotone or boring

Time to prepare:
The "Um" test!

Ask a friend or family member to be your adjudicator in helping you complete this task. Using all of the techniques above, have your adjudicator set a timer for one minute. Get them to ask you the interview questions you have prepared:

- It is your task to say "um", "er", "right" and "ok", as few times as possible.
- It is your adjudicators' task to keep a timer of one minute per question and to keep a tally of the number of time filler words you use.

Remember to breathe slowly, take your time, and use short, tactical pauses.

Practice makes permanent! The more you do it, the more you solidify the responses you have to the questions you will be asked.

Informal Interviewing

I call this the "do I like you?" interview. The informal interview needs preparation just as much as the formal ones do. If you are invited to an informal interview, take into consideration the reasons for this. Be under no illusion – it is to size you up, to check if you fit in and to see whether you should be taken to formal interview. Be prepared and do not leave yourself exposed; be aware of how you behave and consider how you want to be perceived.

Ask insightful questions that demonstrate you have a deep understanding of the job/company for which you are applying. By asking questions you are also showing an interest in the company/organisation whilst also finding out more about the people you could be working with. During informal chats/ interviews, you are likely to be asked the classic interview questions, 'tell me about yourself' etc. Be sure to prepare as if it was a formal interview. Being caught off guard now will result in a trip back to the job boards.

Chapter 7: Ending the Interview

At the end of the interview, the employer will (or should!) ask you, "do you have any questions?" Assuming you still want the job, and you are not planning on just getting up and leaving. This is your opportunity to clear up any misunderstandings and ensure your spot in the list of potential hires.

Be wary of the questions you ask

There is a time and place for asking specific questions. When asked if you have any questions, avoid those regarding potential salary, benefits, or business hours. This information can always be discovered through recruiters prior to interview or negotiated after should you be offered the job. Asking these questions at the end of an interview could be detrimental to the perception the interviewers have of you. Being seen as a someone who is only interested in the money rather than the job itself, does not reflect well on your candidature.

Do not ask questions that have already been answered as these lead hiring managers to believe you have a low attention span and lack listening skills.

Some good questions to ask are:
- "What is the company's expectation of me in the first month/three months?"
- "Which metrics are used to calculate my performance?"
- "What do you like most about the company?"

These questions will show the interviewer, you are interested in understanding the inner workings of the business and aspire to be a high-performing and contributing member of staff.

The 'LGR' technique

Regardless of the job role, seniority, or industry, all of the questions you ask are leading up to "the clarity question" or as I like to call it, the 'LGR' question. In my opinion, this is the only question to ask that truly matters.

LGR Stands for, "Like, Grow, Reservations":

"I LIKE what I have seen today and feel as though *[Company]* is a place I can truly GROW. Do you have any RESERVATIONS about me?"

At the heart of it, the LGR question solicits immediate feedback from the employer without directly asking for it. Essentially, you are using the "like" and the "grow" to soften the "reservations".

Some people may feel it is too rash or forward; I say it shows character and gusto. Consider this: there is no downside to asking this question.

1. If the line manager says, "I have no reservations" then congratulations, you are moving to the next stage in the process.
2. If the line manager has a reservation, this gives you the opportunity to iron out any miscommunications and re-sell yourself as the right candidate.
3. You also come across as a person who is not afraid of feedback and happy to answer difficult questions with grace and humility.

On average, 30% of my clients do not like to ask this question. They either get scared of the answer or do not want to come across as too pushy. However, those who do embrace the LGR technique are glad they did and found it improved their chances at interview.

I cannot stress enough: this is the most important question you need to ask at the end of any interview but make sure you practise your tone of voice when asking this question. You need to sound calm and collected yet enthused and excited about the prospect of working for this company. Own the question, listen to the response, and react appropriately.

Objection handling the reservations

Once you have asked the LGR question, bear in mind, the interviewer may have reservations that they would like to voice and you will need to prepare accordingly.

There are an unquantifiable number of possibilities when it comes to reservations but so long as you approach each reservation with the following formula, you should come back as a stronger candidate in the eyes on the hiring manager.

1. Acknowledge the problem.
2. Show appreciation.
3. Solve and smile.

Below you will find common reservations found at interview, and examples of how to handle them:

"I feel you may be overqualified for the position".

Example answer:
"I understand why you feel I maybe overqualified for this job role and I appreciate your honesty. However, from what I can tell about the business, it is growing and with growth comes

opportunity. I would like the opportunity to prove my worth and grow with the company."

"You did not demonstrate your knowledge in a particular area".

Example answer:
"I understand that I may have not communicated my knowledge in this area thoroughly and I appreciate you giving me the opportunity to put your mind at ease. I have knowledge in [X area] when I worked at [Y]. An example of my experience in this field would be…"

Chapter 8: Group Interviews

Some organisations will use group interviews because they can effectively save time and extract the best candidates from the herd of applicants. The employer's goal is to seek out the candidates who can demonstrate they work well under pressure, are good team players, and fit in with the company's values and culture.

Group interviews are designed to create demand for a position. Having 10–15 interviewees scheduled in for the same interview fosters a sense of competition and places the job role on a metaphorical pedestal, presenting itself as a prize for the victor. The direct outcome of using this hiring technique for the employer is there is less chance of the successful candidate taking a different job at the point of offer, and little to no negotiation of salary involved.

Note: If you feel overqualified for the role, do not let this discourage you or hinder your performance. More often than not, there are multiple job placements within the same company and you may be shortlisted for a higher-level role based on your interview.

Preparing for a Group Interview

Assuming you have researched the company website, found the company's values and learned everything there is to know about the job you are being interviewed for, you will now need to prepare yourself for a full day of assessments and interviews.

Rules of the day:

1. Arrive early

Not too early of course, but certainly early enough to meet reception staff and make a good impression. (Suggestion 10-15 minutes)

2. Engage with everyone

When there are no tasks or interviewers speaking to the group, introduce yourself, engage in small talk and encourage others around you to speak as well. People like people who engage with them first. Ask questions such as "how far did you travel?", "traffic was horrendous, wasn't it?" Anything light and breezy will do but make sure you get the other person talking about themselves.

3. Pay attention at all times

No matter who is talking, listen carefully. It is a long day, and your mind is bound to drift but try to stay focused. Your ability to extract information and relay it back when you are called upon shows a high attention to detail trait that all line managers and HR personnel are looking for.

4. Listen with intent

Consider for a moment; what does good listening look like? I know it sounds strange but good listening is not just something we do with our ears; it has both verbal and non-verbal cues attached to it. For example:
- *Sitting straight in your chair* - this body language show you are interested in what the interviewer has to say.
- *Eye contact* – maintain eye contact based on the 70/50 rule; 70% eye contact while listening and 50% eye contact while speaking.
- *Verbal etiquette* – do not interrupt or talk over the interviewer when they are speaking.

5. Be mindful of your body language

For example, if you know you tend to slouch when seated then make a conscious effort to sit up straight. Sitting upright in your chair gives the impression you are interested and paying attention *[refer chapter 5 for more tips on body language]*.

6. Be competitive but be respectful

Your ability to be competitive without being aggressive or domineering is the most effective way to demonstrate your professionalism within the interview. Allowing other people to shine will show the interviewer you have the ability to work within a team.

7. Never let your guard down

Always keep your discussions professional as you never know who is listening. Some companies may place 'ringers' in group interviews – people who are already employed by the company and who are there to unobtrusively observe and report back on candidates.

Introducing yourself:

This interview usually starts in a room with a mixture of over 10 people consisting of candidates, line managers and HR personnel.

The group interview leader will ask the line managers and company members to stand up, and state their name and position. Now it is your turn. The panel will ask you to state your name to the group and maybe your "claim to fame", or "an interesting fact about yourself". Nothing too strenuous; it is an icebreaker made to make all parties familiar and comfortable.

As part of your preparation, write a few interesting facts and choose which one you would like to use. Something short and sweet will suffice. This is your first opportunity to give a great first impression. Smile, be energetic, enthusiastic and engage the whole room using eye contact.

Tasks on the day:

The tasks chosen on the day of interview will be determined by the key skills, and professional social requirements needed to carry out the job role. Any good human resources department would have sent you an agenda to prepare.

Read the agenda prior to interview. What are the underlying reasons why they are asking you to complete this task? Do they want to see problem-solving skills? Communication skills? Presentation skills? It would be wise to prepare for all contingencies.

If the recruiter has given you too little information for you to determine what tasks lay ahead, do not be afraid to call them and ask for more information.

Practical Group Tasks:

The employer will split you and the other interviewees into small groups, giving each group a time limit to prepare presentations on a specific topic. Then, one by one, each group will present their ideas and plan to the interview panel.

Preparing for an in-house preparation and presentation task is impossible without knowing the subject matter. There are steps and rules to keep in mind if you want to successfully pass this task:

1. **Start with the "why?"**
   Consider why you have been given this task and why this would be beneficial for the organisation. Make your "why" clear at every stage of the presentation.

2. **Do you understand the purpose of the task?**
   An unclear purpose could lead your group in the wrong direction. If you have any uncertainty, simply ask the closest panel member. This shows attention to detail and initiative.

3. **Analyse the task carefully**
   Go through the assignment with a fine toothcomb. What are the most relevant details and facts? Bullet point these details and share them with your group.

4. **Find a unique angle**
   Your competing groups would have found all the simple and obvious facts about the assignments already. Look for unique way of looking at/solving the problem and present that to your team for deliberation.

5. **Map the presentation**
   Mapping out the order of your presentation is key to helping the interview panellists understand your group's point of view. Follow this outline:
   i.   Explain what your group understood from the assignment. "In this task we were asked to…"
   ii.   State the obvious first: "We considered the obvious factors a, b, and c.
   iii. State the group's unique angle: "Our most unique concept of this idea was"

If you find public speaking challenging, holding a power item can be a useful technique to deal with your nerves and anchor you in the moment *(see chapter 4)*.

Note that in these instances, presentation skills are secondary to how you work with others. If you look around, you will see an interview panellist watching and listening to the interaction within your group. The panellists are searching for candidates who are engaging, considerate to other ideas and who can push back on bad ideas constructively and with tact.

When presenting an idea to your group, ask for the opinion of everyone else, engage with every interviewee, and make it clear you are here to collaborate effectively to get the job done. Do not worry if one person presents more information in your group than you; this is a teamwork exercise, not a presentation exercise.

Be considerate and engaging

When I first started out my career within recruiting, I was invited to a group interview with over 40 candidates, all competing for one of five recruitment consultant positions within a small firm. I spent six hours in this group interview. Seven tasks were assigned including: self-presentation, group presentation and group team building.

One of our tasks was, "In groups of six, discuss then present the downsides of failing to give unsuccessful applicants feedback". I enthusiastically smiled, picked up the pen and with outstretched hand said, "Who wants to write?"

During the process of writing, I was offering out ideas and suggesting the direction of the presentation, all while engaging with each individual and asking for their feedback.

One group member randomly and rudely said, "We don't like your ideas!". I was taken aback and did not understand what I had done to make him so upset. Nevertheless, I smiled, apologised if I was talking too much, and asked if he had any other ideas.

What we did not realise is that one of the interview panellists was sitting next to him and was now frowning at his comment. Subsequently he did not get the job, but I and two other members of my team did.

I share this anecdote as a warning to be considerate of those around you and if you receive negative or unnecessary feedback from a group member, always maintain your dignity and professionalism as it can only reflect well on you.

Role-Playing Tasks

Role-playing exercises are some of the trickiest group interview tasks you will be asked to take part in. Placing you in a hypothetical scenario can be difficult but let us break it down and consider the purpose of a role-playing exercise. Ultimately the employer would like to see how well you communicate within a particular scenario based on the job for which you have applied.

The interviewer is therefore assessing candidates for their problem-solving ability, communication skills and critical thinking. Your most valuable tools in this scenario are your ears; listen to the problem and ask probing questions to gather further information.

Scenario Example:
You work in a bank. A customer (played by the interviewer)

has walked into the bank and is complaining about missing money from their account. The customer is not up to date with modern technology and therefore has not been using the new systems in place to support customers with online banking. The customer is referred to as a "traditional" client and prefers face to face interaction instead of using technology. Recently, this customer has complained about not understanding why the bank has changed their systems and demands to speak to someone because "the old system works better".

In this scenario, you will need to show your ability to use critical thinking and ask relevant and engaging questions in order to understand the situation in more detail. Communication will be key to solving the problem and therefore speaking in an appropriate manner according to the behaviour of the interviewer is crucial. To ensure that the problem is solved properly, you will need to consider a variety of solutions that can help the customer moving forward.

Chapter 9: Presentation Interviews

A pre-determined presentation will be about a specific subject matter to discuss e.g. "what innovative change methodology would you bring to your team in order to help team members perform better?".

It is easy to get carried away with big and costly ideas to present in your interview but try to resist. The simplest ideas tend to be the most effective. Do not try to reinvent the wheel.

Your presentation can be broken down into five pillars of understanding:

1. **What is the message you want to send?**
   Make it clear from the start what the purpose of the presentation is – the "why" that is at the core of your idea or subject. Link this to a key message that you will use throughout your presentation. Start and finish your presentation with your message in mind.

2. **Plan your timing:**
   Interview presentations have set timing guidelines, usually between 15–20 minutes. This is more than enough time to get your message across to the interview panel. You must practice and time yourself to ensure you are within the correct timelines and have followed the guidance exactly.

3. **Be wary of "information overload":**
   You will need your pitch to be rich in information and facts but also precise and to the point. Do not fill your presentation with too much text or imagery as it will cognitively overload the panel and your message may be

lost. Similarly, avoid merely repeating what you have written on the presentation slides. You want to keep the panel focussed on you and what you are saying, so use key bullet points with as few words as possible on your slides and elaborate on the rest verbally. You can develop a script for yourself to help you flesh out the details of your ideas during the presentation without relying on text-heavy slides which will distract and detract your audience from focussing on you.

4. Back up your concepts:
Backing up your concepts and ideas with previously conducted research and studies is a great way of gaining the attention and buy-in from the employer. It shows the employer you have comprised your presentation from evidence and facts. For example, "In a study conducted by [Institution, university or professional] ...". Your research must be conducted prior to interview and include information you have gathered from the recruiter and employer website.

5. Memorise and familiarise
Read your content, script and slides repeatedly so that you become in harmony with your content. This will minimise mind blanks and help with your presentation flow.

Structuring your presentation:
You may be tempted to go straight to "fingers on keyboard" and just start typing up your presentation but good planning is required to ensure you keep your audience engaged and communicate your point effectively.

Once you have come up with the message you want to

convey, choose a route for storytelling. Every narrative has a beginning, middle and end and there are several different storytelling formulas you can deploy to keep your audience engaged and interested.

Storytelling formulas:

1. **Situation - Fact – Story – Repeat – Reward**
   Situation: Reaffirm the current realities of the situation, scenario, or task. Invite the panel to consider a hypothetical new reality- what "could be" a better way of doing things?
   Fact: "What are the facts?" Summarise the facts of the situation.
   Story: "What could be?" Present a clear scenario of how your ideas could become the new reality and reveal your proposed plans.
   Repeat: Repeat the fact and story until you are ready to end.
   Reward: End with a call to action to reap the rewards of your proposal.

This structure dips between the two questions posed and answered by the presenter; "what is?" and "what could be?". This style of presentation is good for providing solid information to the interviewer while presenting your solutions. A good example of this storytelling formula is used by David McCandless in his Ted Talk; the beauty of data visualisations where he keeps the audience in a state of "wanting more".

2. **Situation – Complication– Resolution**
   Situation: simply states the situation without the problem then adds *"however"* e.g. "Our company currently uses agile project management

methodologies, *however...*"

Complication: An extension to the situation which outlines the problem or complication e.g. "Our company currently uses agile project management methodologies; *however,* the evidence shows it is compromising quality of work."

Resolution: The connection from the problem to the solution using "therefore" e.g.

"Our Company currently uses 'agile' to project manage IT integrations; *however,* the evidence shows it is compromising the quality of work. *Therefore,* to stabilise the quality we need to change our methodologies to 'waterfall'."

Follow up questions

Try to predict the follow up questions the interview panel will be asking you at the end. Look at your ideas objectively; what questions would you ask if you on the receiving end of this presentation? Consider using the following prompts to help structure the questions:

- "If scenario (a) would happen, how would you go about using your solution to resolve this?"
- "In what timeline do you feel you could implement your idea?"
- "What problems do you foresee?"

Chapter 10: Interviewing for a Higher Position

Often, the interview process for a higher position involves multiple stages. The first round may be with the direct line manager and HR representative. Shortlisted candidates who reach the final round may then be asked to attend subsequent interviews; usually, these interviews take the form of one-to-one meetings with a director or senior leadership member.

What is important to remember when interviewing with a director; the emphasis is usually on your personality and character attributes. They may have specific questions for you or want to hear about your career background but often the reality is they just want to get a feel for whether they like you and if they see you as a good fit for the position.

One of the scariest steps in my career was taking the leap from team member to team manager. I was sitting in the interview room waiting for the finance director of a new company to meet me. I was nervous and all I could think about was, "How am I going to speak to the director and show him I could do a job I have never done before?". I was suffering from a classic case of 'imposter syndrome' *[see chapter 3].*

The director greeted me with a half-smile and a squint of curiosity. He sat up in his chair with a long list of questions at the ready. I glanced at his page and noticed the letters 'HR' in the top right-hand corner. This told me he had been supplied with a line of questioning by his human resources team. In that moment I remember feeling elation and relief; he had not prepared his own detailed line of questioning - and I could use this to my advantage.

For every question the director asked me, I had a follow up question for him. Four questions later, we were speaking about his vision for the company over the next six months, his long-term plans and even a mutual interest in sport. Instead of the interrogation I had initially feared, the interview had become a conversation. By the end, we were making plans for the future of the business together and I got the job.

What I had done is "flip the interview" and established a rapport with my interviewer. Flipping the interview is a technique used to take the spotlight away from you and turn the interview into a conversation about the interviewer. This works in one-on-one scenarios, however, if you are dealing with a highly process-driven interviewer, this can be a much trickier technique to use as the person must want to talk about themselves.

Flipping the interview is a difficult technique to master but when used correctly and on the right person, you will find yourself in the driving seat of the interview. I was taught this technique from an old mentor of mine who explained that "building rapport doesn't come from the best answers; it comes from the best questions."

Using this technique must feel natural and you will need to prepare your own line of questioning prior to interview.

1. **Research the person who is interviewing you**.
   Go on to LinkedIn, find the person and check how long they have been with the company. If it is a short time, they will be enthusiastic to prove themselves and have lots of plans to talk about. Ask about those plans. If the interviewer has been at the company for a long time,

they will hold a deep understanding of the company's needs and problems. Probe the interviewer about the company's needs and discuss possible solutions.

2. **Find the pain and press:**
   This is a common sales technique but when applied to an interview situation it breaks down barriers and hands you the keys to drivers' seat. In your questions, you must quickly find out what problem you will be solving if hired i.e. "What are the current issues within the department?". This gives you the opportunity to offer solutions or experiences where you have solved such problems in the past. Overall, issues usually fall within the following trend: the current process takes too long which slows productivity and produces minimal results.

3. **Do not interrupt; respond.**
   It may be tempting to agree with the interviewer and interrupt whilst they are talking. DO NOT do this. While the interviewer is talking, smile, nod, analyse and respond once they have finished speaking. By listening in full you are also allowing yourself time to find the next question to ask them.

Questions to consider asking:
- What systems are you using to manage tasks?
- How are those systems working to manage your processes?
- Are those systems delivering the results you are hoping for?
- What are the current processes in place to help navigate that situation?
- What do you think of the team?

- What are your plans over the next six months for the department?
- What is the number one issue that you would like to solve in this department?

Chapter 11: Salary Negotiations

"You do not get what you want. You get what you negotiate".
- Harvey Mackay

A 2012 study by salary.com revealed; "18% of people never negotiate on salary, 44% never approached the subject during performance review, while only 37% of people say they always negotiate."

There are two types of people when it comes to negotiations: the person who sets boundaries and knows their worth, or the person who is too uncomfortable or embarrassed to negotiate. Know your worth!

First rule is to check your ambitions. When asking for a salary increase within a company, nine times out of 10, you are likely to receive a maximum 5% rise, whereas moving from company to company can warrant up to and over a 15%–20% increase, depending on your negotiation strategy.

DISCLAIMER: DO NOT JOB HOP
Wanting a higher salary and moving from job to job to get to a higher salary makes you a 'job-hopper'. This puts you at the bottom of the CV pile when applying for a new job. Before moving from one permanent role to the next, you need to consider the length of time you have been working for one company.

As a rule of thumb, you should be working for two years within one company before moving on to the next. Any less and the next employer will feel as though you hold no loyalty to the companies you work with. That said, there is such a thing as too much loyalty. If you stay within a company for over 6–8 years, hiring companies may consider this a negative. Very long-standing job roles suggests personality traits that are associated with a fear of change. Aim to move job roles every 2–3 years to hit the salary rise and reputation sweet spot. If your CV shows you have taken a number of jobs over a short period of time, be sure to have a credible explanation ready to ease any suspicions the recruiter may have. Likewise, if you have been working the same company for several years, demonstrating you had received appropriate promotions every few years would go some way to alleviating concerns that you lack ambition or appetite for change.

Negotiating after receiving a job offer

Negotiating starts from the moment you receive the first stage interview invitational phone call. This is where you start your planning and preparation.

You need the following information to put you in a position of strength:
- Why are they hiring for this role?
- How long have they been looking?
- Are you replacing someone?
- Is it a new position?
- What is the budget for this position?

The answers to these questions will give you a clear picture about how important the correct hire is for the position. If the recruiter says they simply do not have the budget to pay the salary you are asking for, consider this as a red flag. If the company does not have the budget to pay you what you are worth, cut and run! A growing company will have no problem investing in good talent and will be open to negotiations.

In some cases, line managers are so underpaid that their subordinates suffer lower salaries as a consequence. This is often due to company policy set in place to maintain a sufficient pay gap between managers and team members. Again, avoid a company like this as it indicates they cannot see the value of their employees and prefer to keep them at low salaries for as long as possible.

They want to hire you and are asking "how much?"

What do you bring to the table? Are you 100% confident you can fulfil all the requirements? If the company is hiring, they have done their research and are aware of the market standards. Likewise, you should ensure you know the market standards and set yourself a target salary. It is always better to start high; once you have chosen your target salary, increase it by 15% to 20%, this will give you a negotiation buffer. Do not be afraid to refuse an offer that does not meet your lowest number. Accepting a job that does not meet your present-day ambitions will discourage and demotivate you.

It is more than likely you will have a mediator (external/internal recruiter) that will set up interviews, perform standard skill investigations and negotiate on your behalf. Internal recruiters have the ears of the line-managers and directors of the business. Creating a good bond with this person will give you extra negotiating power at the end of the hiring process.

Negotiating with external recruiters

Contract role negotiations

When a hiring company has a short-term project to complete, they have two main options concerning hiring: either they can use a consultancy company or hire a contractor via an external recruitment agency.

A consultancy company will assign a member of their team who specialises in the project requested by the hiring company, whereas an external recruiter will source a candidate and account manage a contractor. Recruitment agencies are assigned a budget and their fee will sit within that budget.

Example: "Company X" is hiring a Business Analyst for a six-month contract. They assign a budget of £500 a day for the entirety of that contract. "Company X" contacts a recruitment agency to find the candidate they need.

What many people do not know about accepting a contract role is; the recruitment agency wants to keep as much of this budget in their pocket as possible. Therefore, the recruiter will offer £350 a day to the candidate, keeping £150 per day as part of their fee. The hiring company are indirectly paying the day rate via the recruitment agency. In these cases, negotiation should always start with the recruitment agency, not the hiring company. It is essential to negotiate the contract day rate every three months or when the contract is up for renewal.

Permanent role negotiations

Contrary to contract negotiations, recruitment agencies are motivated to give you the highest salary possible and will negotiate on your behalf to get you the best possible outcome. The recruitment agencies fee is separate to your salary. They are paid a finder's fee based on 15-25% of your starting salary. With external recruiters, just be clear from the beginning as to your salary expectations and they will relay the information.

Asking for a salary increase whilst currently working for a company

Undoubtedly, your line manager has a budget to stick to and giving you a pay rise is not something they account for, nor want to take out of their budget.

Be prepared

Do not ambush your line manager. You will need a plan of action. Before your next one-to-one meeting, request a performance review, then begin stating your case. Keep in mind that the cost of hiring someone new far outweighs the cost of a 5% incremental rise you are requesting.

Do your research

Find out if the salary for your current job role sits within the lower, mid or higher band of the market salary grading. You can check this by using www.salary.com / www.payscale.com or by simply looking for your role on job websites and seeing how much other companies are paying their employees within similar positions. I strongly advise that you analyse your situation against the higher job specification and be realistic; request a 5% increment but be happy with 2.5%.

Do you deserve the pay rise?

You will have been at the company for over a year before

considering a salary negotiation. Re-read your job description and ask yourself if you meet all the criteria? More importantly, are you exceeding expectations? This is important information you need to state your case to your line manager, alongside any data that suggests the impact you have had within the company to warrant a salary increase.

List your achievements

Make a bragging list: pretend your best friend is fighting your corner. What would they say about your work? Do you always meet deadlines? Have you been working late? Do you take on extra responsibilities? Do you go "above and beyond"?

Get it in writing!

Verbal promises are a fool's contract and about as useful as a book with blank pages. John is a friend of mine and when he was looking for a job, I was the Head of Talent Acquisition for a large multinational company. My recommendation, therefore, held weight and the director was happy to speak with him. The director that interviewed him was impressed and wanted to proceed with the hire. When it came to the job offer stage, John was offered £48,000. However, it was agreed verbally that this would rise to £50,000 after John had passed his six-month probation.

Once John had passed his probation period, he asked for the £2,000 rise. However, lo-and behold the director could not remember agreeing to the pay rise. John spent a further four months pushing for the pay rise before the director gave in and authorised it. Don't get caught out like this! If a similar offer is made to you, make sure you get it in writing.

The devil is in the counteroffer

After telling your current place of work you are resigning your post to join another company, they may tempt you back with a counteroffer. Receiving a counteroffer from your current workplace is flattering and makes you feel valued. DO NOT TAKE IT.

The company that has provided you a counteroffer has done so because they are now in a position of pain. By letting you go right now, they will lack the resources to complete urgent projects and fall behind. However, now that you have shown a lack of loyalty to the company you will be treated in kind. If a rainy day comes and redundancies are on the table, you will likely be one of the first to go.

On average 80% of people who take a counteroffer, leave the company 3-6 months after accepting. Yes, you have a little more money in your pocket, but the reasons why you wanted to leave in the first place are still there.

Chapter 12: Interview Checklist

Assuming you have thoroughly prepared for your interview, here is a checklist which applies to all types of interviews. Be sure to follow the guide. This has helped many of my clients to remain calm and collected in the face of a challenging interview.

Company research:
Never underestimate the value of learning more about the company. What is the company's ethos? What are its values and vision? What key words that are used throughout the website? Make note of these so you can reference them in interview and demonstrate how you are aligned to them. Look

at their news feed; have they completed any projects recently? If appropriate, comment on how impressed you are with regards to their projects, but, be sure to check the date on the articles as they may no longer be relevant to current projects.

Interviewer research:

Do not forget to research who is interviewing you. A simple LinkedIn search usually does the trick. This can give you all sorts of valuable information such as length of company service, a breakdown of their responsibilities and their work history.

The "night before" prep:

Make sure you have prepared everything you will need the night before your interview; clothes laid out, job specification printed and journey plan all worked out. Waking up prepared for every aspect of the interview allows you to focus your thoughts on the task ahead.

Getting an early night may sound cliché but when our bodies do not get enough REM (rapid eye movement) sleep, it can compromise our decision-making, processing skills and hinder our creativity. According to a report by the National Institute of Neurological Disorders and Stroke, a lack of sleep affects our memory, performance and ability to think clearly[11]. So, YES; get an early night!

---

[11] National Institute of Neurological Disorders and Stroke, *'Brain Basics: Understanding Sleep"*, https://www.ninds.nih.gov/Disorders/Patient-Caregiver-Education/Understanding-Sleep

Morning before Interview prep:

1. ***Hydration*** Drink two cups of water before your morning coffee. This hydrates your brain and allows you to focus.

2. ***Have a light breakfast***
   When your body is digesting a large quantity of food, it will put your body in a state of "postprandial somnolence"– also known as a 'food coma' - thereby reducing your focus and concentration levels.

3. ***Allow plenty of time***
   Leave for your interview with plenty of time and arrive no later than 15 minutes before the appointment. The last thing you need is to feel lateness anxiety.

Final Thoughts

"Sometimes you win, sometimes you learn."
- John Maxwell
-

Thank you for taking the time to read "Prepare to be Hired". I am confident if you follow the preparation techniques set out in this guide, you will find success at interview - especially for those jobs deemed hard-to-reach.

Bear in mind, however, not all job interviews are in your control. Sometimes you can spend days preparing for one interview only to find the company already had an internal candidate ear-marked for the job. While this can be demoralising, I assure you that it happens to the best of us. It is not the end of the world and the preparation you have completed is invaluable for the next interview you attend. Never be disheartened by an unsuccessful interview and do not give up on your ambitions. Practice makes progress. Practice makes permanent.

About the Author

Marios Zenonos is a high impact, astute and strategic former Talent Acquisition Head, with over 10 years' experience working within both private and public sectors for global and SME businesses. He has a proven track record of building successful recruitment, learning and development functions from the ground up.

He launched Enterview, a life and career coaching consultancy service in 2019. Highly passionate and attentive, Marios has a natural ability to motivate and support clients to perform at their best. For more information visit www.EnterView.co.uk.

Prepare
- To Be -
Hired

MARIOS ZENONOS

Special Thanks
Kevin Liddle

Jaquelin Liddle

Racheal Frank

Soula Hagge

Zena Zenonos

Printed in Great Britain
by Amazon

87108455R00047